50

Animal Crafts

for Little Kids

Georgina Bomer

50 Animal Crafts for Little Kids

by Georgina Bomer

ISBN-13: 978-1507656082
ISBN-10: 1507656084

Adult supervision is recommended for every project featured in this book. Please read the instructions for each activity thoroughly before deciding whether it is appropriate for your child(ren). The author is not responsible for any injury or damage while replicating activities from this book.

https://craftulate.com/
https://georginabomer.com/

Photography by Georgina Bomer

Other books by this author:
Art, Craft and Cooking with Toddlers
99 Fine Motor Ideas (co-author)
The Dieter's Chocolate Cookbook

Contents

Introduction

This book was written for parents, teachers and caregivers who would like to do fun and easy animal crafts with children. The book is separated into chapters for different animal categories, but there is some crossover between the sections so I recommend that you read it all!

Ages

The crafts in this book are suitable for children aged 2-5. Most crafts give a wide scope in terms of how much a child can participate, depending on age and ability. I have not specified exact ages for each activity as I think it is best to determine this on an individual basis. If you are crafting with children of mixed ages then you may like to get the older children to prepare some of the crafts for the younger ones. Please take extra care with any crafts that involve scissors and/or pipe cleaners.

Templates

Several of the crafts require an adult to freehand an animal shape but you will also find the internet a huge source of basic outlines. The majority of the templates I have used in the book were found on Clker.com.

Reducing Mess and Quick Clean Up

Art and crafts can get messy, but there are ways to minimize this. For example, I always have a box of baby wipes to hand. I often use painters' tape to secure the paper or card to the table. And for quick clean up I love using disposable bowls or plates as paint trays - especially when I am working with a group of children.

Glue and Paint

Many crafts in this book use glue and/or paint. I would highly recommend finding a good source of both that is washable. If you do not like the potential for mess that comes with glue, you may prefer to use glue dots.

Craft Materials

Most of the crafts featured in this book use standard craft materials - I particularly LOVE to use recyclables when crafting! These are the most commonly used materials in the book:

- Empty cardboard tubes (either kitchen towel or toilet paper)

- Paper and card

- Marker pens

- Paper plates

- Googly eyes

In fact, you will see googly eyes featured on nearly EVERY craft. And those that don't feature it could easily have them added! There's a good reason for this. Googly eyes immediately add character and bring the craft to life. Above is a very basic example for you. These are play dough animals (p34) made using cookie cutters. By simply adding a googly eye it changes them completely!

Zoo
Animals

Marble Painted Tiger

Materials:

- White cardstock

- Orange and black paint

- Marbles

- Deep baking dish, tray, or container

- Scissors

Print a blank outline of a tiger onto some white cardstock – a quick internet search brings up several you could use. Alternatively, freehand draw the outline onto the card.

Tape the tiger picture down to the inside of a deep baking dish and add a few squirts of orange and black paint at the top of the picture. This is to try and encourage a vertical stripe design. You may like to add more of the orange paint so that the black paint doesn't take over! Place a marble in each puddle of orange paint.

Then it is time to get rolling! Show your child how to tilt the baking dish to move the marbles over the card. Try and get as much paint coverage over the tiger as you can. Once the paint has dried, cut it out and add back any features that have been painted over.

To finish the project, glue the tiger onto a green background made by using the same marble painting method!

Paper Bag Elephant Puppet

Materials:

- Brown paper bag
- Gray or brown craft foam or card
- White craft foam or card
- Pink craft foam or card
- Scissors
- Glue
- Marker pens

Prepare the craft by drawing the required shapes on the craft foam or card. Two large ears in gray, two tusks and two eyes in white, a trunk in gray and inner ear pieces in pink. Remember to add in a little tab on the joining side of the large ears to fit into the fold of the paper bag.

Cut out all the pieces (or ask your child to do it if they are old enough). Draw on extra details to the eyes and trunk if required.

Show your child how to glue on all the pieces to complete the elephant.

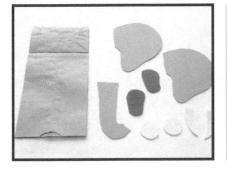

Reindeer Ornament

Materials:

- Styrofoam ball
- Googly eyes
- Red pom pom
- Brown and red pipe cleaners
- Black felt
- Bell
- Ribbon and pin
- Wire cutters and scissors

Prepare the brown pipe cleaners by using the wire cutters to cut them into quarters. Do not use scissors for cutting pipe cleaners! Bend the pipe cleaners into two antler shapes.

Provide your child with all the other materials. The bell will need to be threaded onto the red pipe cleaner, and a mouth shape cut out of the black felt.

Show your child how to push both ends of the red pipe cleaner into the ball to form a bell collar, and push in the antlers at the top. Then glue on the eyes, nose and mouth. Push the pin through the ribbon and into the top of the ball, tie a knot, and hang on your tree!

Use the softer type of Styrofoam ball (with the rough surface) for this craft.

Animal Craft Stick Puzzle

Materials:

- Animal picture*
- Scissors
- Glue
- 10 craft sticks
- Craft knife
- Cutting mat
- Wire cutters and scissors

The animal picture can be cut from a magazine or old catalog. This orangutan picture was cut from an old calendar.

Cut out the animal picture in a square, approximately 4.25 x 4.25". Spread glue onto the back of the picture and carefully line up the craft sticks onto the glue, leaving a small gap between each one.

When the glue has dried, use a craft knife on a cutting mat to cut between the craft sticks. This is definitely a task for an adult!

The puzzle can be as easy or hard as you'd like to make it depending on the picture you choose!

Although this craft is included in the Zoo Animals section - it really can be made with any picture or photo!

Egg Carton Camel

Materials:

- Cardboard egg carton
- Scissors
- Brown paint
- Clothespins
- Googly eyes
- Glue

Cut out a section of three cups for each camel. Trim the edges. This is actually trickier than it sounds and takes far longer than you might think!

Attach four clothespins to the corners of two adjacent cups, leaving one on the end free to make the head. Adjust the clothespins so that all legs are level and touch the ground.

Paint the egg carton and clothespins with brown paint. This can get messy! To finish, glue on a googly eye.

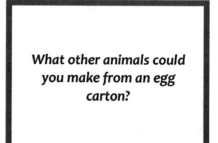

What other animals could you make from an egg carton?

Cardboard Tube Lion

Materials:

- Empty cardboard tube
- Yellow and orange paint
- Paintbrush
- White paper
- Yellow marker pen
- Scissors
- Black marker pen
- Tape or glue
- Orange pipe cleaner

Using the yellow and orange paint, encourage your child to paint the cardboard tube. With the leftover paint, suggest that they paint on the white paper. Once the paint has dried, give them a yellow pen to scribble over the paint to form the lion's mane.

From the paper, cut out a head shape and draw on the lion's facial features. Use scissors to make small cuts around the edge, then ruffle them to give it some texture. Glue or tape the head to the top of the tube.

Make a hole in the base of the tube at the back and thread an orange pipe cleaner through to make a tail.

Cutting the lion's mane can be great fine motor skills practice for preschoolers!

Rice Covered Polar Bear

Materials:

- White paper
- Marker pen
- Scissors
- Glue
- Colored card
- Paint brush
- White rice

Use the marker pen to draw an outline of a polar bear onto the white paper. The internet can be a very useful source of templates if you don't feel comfortable drawing it freehand.

Cut out the bear and glue it onto some colored card. Depending on the ability of your child they may like to help at this stage.

Spread glue onto the bear with a brush, then invite your child to sprinkle rice onto the glue until the polar bear is covered. Shake off any excess rice, and patch holes if required. To secure the rice further, brush another layer of glue over the top once the initial glue has dried.

If you prefer not to use food in your crafts then shredded paper would make a great alternative!

Paper Plate Snake

Materials:

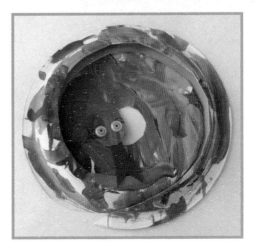

- Paper plate
- Paint
- Scissors
- Red card or paper
- Glue
- Googly eyes

This craft is very versatile! You could use any size or color of paper plate, and any color of paint! Just invite them to paint the back of the plate however they would like.

Once the paint has dried, cut a long spiral into the plate, ending with a head shape. This is probably a job for an adult.

Cut a forked tongue shape from the red card or paper and glue it onto the head. To finish, glue on some googly eyes.

Try printing with bubble wrap for some interesting textures on the snake!

Shape Monkey

Materials:

- Brown card in two shades

- Scissors

- Glue

- Marker pen

- 3 brown pipe cleaners

- Wire cutters

Cut a large and medium circle from the darker brown card. Bowls, plates and cups make useful circle templates! From the lighter brown card, cut two small circles, one heart and one oval. This can be done by an older child or an adult.

Show your child how to glue the two dark brown circles together so they slightly overlap. Add ears to each side of the head. For the face, glue the heart to the bottom of the circle then glue the oval over the top.

Cut two brown pipe cleaners in half, and tape them to the back of the monkey to form arms and legs. With the third pipe cleaner, curl it up at one end then tape it to the back to form the tail.

This craft is a great opportunity to talk about different shapes.

Foam Cup Zebra

Materials:

- Styrofoam cup
- Black and white pipe cleaners
- Wire cutters
- Black card
- Scissors
- Googly eyes
- Glue

To prepare the craft, twist together a black and white pipe cleaner. Repeat two more times. Cut one of the pipe cleaner twists in half using the wire cutters (don't use scissors!). Cut one of the halves into half again. Bend the little quarter pieces into loops that will form the ears.

From the black paper, cut out some stripes and a nose. Show your child how to glue these onto the cup, and then add the eyes. Push the pipe cleaners into the cup: the two ears, the two long twists for the legs and the half length for a tail.

This zebra craft looks very cute sitting on a shelf or ledge!

Ocean Animals and Fish

Marbled Animal Ocean Art

Materials:

- White shaving cream
- Shallow dishes
- Acrylic paint
- Stirring stick (like a chopstick!)
- White card (cut to fit inside the dishes)
- Plastic scraper tool / putty knife
- Animal cookie cutters
- Marker pens

Spray a thin layer of the shaving cream into the dish, then add a few drops of paint. Start with only a few colors – you can always add more later!

Swirl the colors around with a stick to make a marble pattern. Carefully lay a piece of card over the top of the paint and cream mixture, gently push down, and then lift off the card.

Leave the mixture on the card for a minute or two, then use the scraper tool to remove the excess shaving cream (I wiped it onto some kitchen paper for easy clean-up).

After the prints have dried, use animal cookie cutters as stencils to cut out shapes, and use the pens to add details.

This technique can also be used for making gift wrap!

Mesh Print Sea Turtle

Materials:

- Plastic mesh scourer
- Green paint
- White card
- Green card
- Scissors
- Glue
- Googly eyes

Invite your child to dip the scourer into the green paint and make prints all over the white card.

When it has dried, cut a large oval shape from the white card. Then cut shapes from the green card: a head, a tail, and four flippers.

Glue the body parts onto the white card, and add googly eyes.

Textured Starfish

Materials:

- Starfish outline*
- White card
- Glue
- O-shaped cereal
- Grains or sand

*Draw one freehand or print out a template from the internet.

Spread the glue onto the starfish outline. Invite your child to cover the glue in o-shaped cereal. They can place them carefully in rows or randomly.

Then fill in the gaps with the grains or sand. Encourage them to take little pinches of the grain and sprinkle over the glue - this will give them some fine motor practice too!

After the glue has dried, shake off any excess. Cover with another layer of glue to help preserve the artwork.

Star shaped "pastina" looks very cute in this craft!

Paper Plate Fish

Materials:

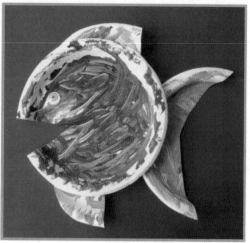

- Two white paper plates
- Paint and paintbrushes
- Scissors
- Googly eyes
- Glue
- Tape

Invite your child to paint the plates however they would like. We often use paper plates as paint trays so this is a perfect way to turn them into a craft.

Once the paint has dried, cut a mouth shape from one of the plates, and then fins and tail from the other plate.

Attach as shown using a combination of glue and tape - whichever works for your type of plates.

Ask your child to glue on the googly eye!

Paper Plate Lobster

Materials:

- Red paper plate (or you could paint a white one with red paint)
- Scissors
- Craft knife and cutting surface
- Brads (paper fasteners)
- Googly eyes
- Red pipe cleaner
- Glue

Cut two claws from the sides of the plate as shown, and use the center section for the body.

Use a craft knife to make holes in the ends of the claws and "arms" and push a brad through to secure them together.

Make another hole at the top of the body and thread the pipe cleaner through.

Then glue on some tiny googly eyes!

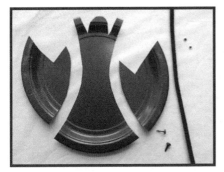 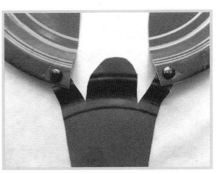

Cardboard Tube Octopus

Materials:

- Empty cardboard tube*
- Paint and paintbrush
- Scissors
- Googly eyes
- Glue
- Marker pen

*You can use either a kitchen paper tube or a toilet paper tube for this craft

Paint the cardboard tube. Octopuses are often represented as purple creatures   maybe because there aren't enough purple animals!

When the paint has dried, cut lengthways up the tube to form eight sections. Curl up each cut section to form the tentacles.

Glue on the googly eyes and draw on a mouth.

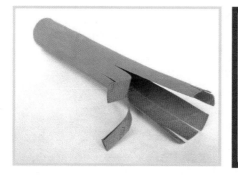

You could also paint the underside of the tentacles - perhaps with a different color?

Paint Swatch Fish

Materials:

- Card
- Scissors
- Paint swatches*
- Circle paper punch
- Glue
- Googly eye

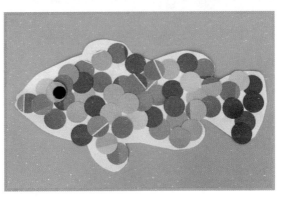

If you don't already have old paint swatches please ask your DIY store first before taking the swatches, or you could even ask if they have any out of date swatches you could have.

Cut a fish shape out of the card. Prepare the "scales" by using the circle paper punch on the paint swatches. Depending on the age and ability of the child they can help with this – it is great fine motor practice as it works on hand strength!

Spread the glue onto the card and invite your child to place the colored circles onto the glue. Once they have covered the fish, add a googly eye to finish.

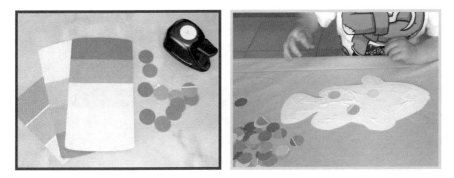

Party Bowl Jellyfish

Materials:

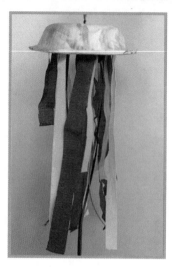

- Paper party bowl
- Watercolor paint
- Paintbrush
- Scissors
- Ribbon, yarn, strips of crepe paper, strips of tissue paper
- Glue

Use watercolor paints to color the outside of the bowl. Kids can use any combination of colors for this!

Once the paint has dried, make a hole in the center of the bowl and thread a loop of ribbon through. Tie a knot to secure it.

Spread glue into the middle of the bowl and invite your child to add the strips of ribbon, yarn and paper. You may need to add more glue if the original amount gets covered.

Hang up the jellyfish from the ribbon loop.

Farm
Animals

Yarn Wrap Sheep

Materials:

- Card
- Scissors
- Glue
- Marker pens
- Black yarn
- Tape

Cut out a sheep outline from two pieces of card, gluing them back to back but not joining the legs together. This gives the card extra stability and then the legs can be separated at the end so that the sheep can stand up. Draw on features if required.

Tape one end of the yarn to the sheep and show your child how to wrap the yarn around the body of the sheep. This takes quite a bit of co-ordination for younger children and is great fine motor practice, too!

Once the sheep is covered in yarn, secure the end by tucking it into the wrapped yarn, then open out the legs so that the sheep can stand up.

If you use black yarn as shown here you could sing "Baa Baa Black Sheep" while you wrap the sheep!

Farm Animal Handprints

Materials:

- Card or paper

- Paint

- Paintbrush

- Marker pens

- Googly eyes and glue (optional)

Cow Handprint: White handprint on colored card or paper. Add black and pink details with QTips.

Pig Handprint: Pink handprint on white paper. Add ears and snout made from pink paper or card. Draw on eyes and nostrils or glue on googly eyes.

Horse Handprint: Brown handprint on white paper. Draw on mane, tail, hooves and head details with marker pen.

Duckling Handprint: Yellow handprint on white paper. Cut out and glue onto colored card. Use a marker pen to draw on wing, beak, eye and feet details.

These would make a lovely wall decoration for your child's bedroom!

Paper Plate Pig

Materials:

- White paper plate
- Small plastic cup
- Glue
- Pink paint
- Paintbrush
- Pink, white and black card
- Scissors

Prepare the craft by gluing the plastic cup to the paper plate. Then invite your child to paint the whole thing pink.

Once the paint has dried, cut out some pink triangles for ears, black ovals for nostrils, and some black and white circles for eyes.

Invite your child to glue on the pieces. If you want a less abstract look you can put the glue on for them, or even use glue dots. However you may prefer to just let your child place the card wherever they like!

Circle paper punches are useful for cutting out neat circles for the eyes.

Play Dough Animals

Materials:

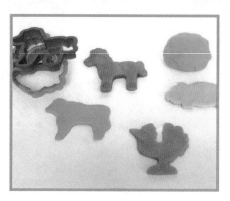

- 1/2 cup AP flour

- 1/2 cup water

- 2 tbs salt

- 1 tsp cream of tartar

- 2-3 drops food dye

- Animal shaped cookie cutters

To make homemade play dough add the flour, water, salt, and cream of tartar to a non- stick saucepan and stir well to mix. Add food dye until you get the desired color.

Heat slowly, stirring regularly. The mixture will start to thicken, and then pull away from the sides of the saucepan. After about five minute the mixture will have formed into a ball.

Place the dough on some wax paper, let cool slightly, then knead until smooth. Make several batches with different colors for varied play.

Flatten out the dough with your child (use a rolling pin or their hand!) and let them press the cookie cutters into it to form the animals.

This "taste-safe" play dough is suitable for even the youngest toddlers.

Rocking Paper Plate Rooster

Materials:

- White paper plate

- Red and yellow craft foam or card

- Glue

- Googly eyes

- White feathers

Fold the paper plate in half.

Cut out a wattle and comb shape from the red craft foam (or card), and a beak from the yellow. Glue into position, then add a googly eye.

Glue on some white feathers over the body of the rooster. You could also convert this craft into a hen, chicken, or any other kind of bird!

The rooster will rock if you push down on one side!

Scrunched Paper Cow

Materials:

- White card

- Pencil or cow outline template

- Black, white and pink tissue paper

- Glue

- Googly eyes

Draw a cow head onto the white card or print out a template from the internet.

Give small pieces of black tissue paper to your child, and show them how to scrunch them up into little balls. Spread glue on the areas that you want to be black, and show them how to glue them on. Repeat for the white and pink tissue paper.

Glue on the googly eyes to finish. Alternatively, cut out holes for the eyes and turn this into a mask! Either attach string to go around your child's head or glue on a large craft stick for a hand-held mask.

The detail of the cow can be as simple or as complicated as you like!

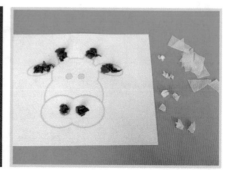

Straw Printed Lamb

Materials:

- Black card
- White paint
- Drinking straw
- Scissors
- Googly eyes
- Glue

Show your child how to dip the end of the drinking straw into the white paint and make prints on the black paper, encourage them to fill the page. If they are not used to printing activities then you may have to show them how to use only the end of the straw, rather than sweep with it like a paintbrush.

After the paint has dried, cut out an outline of a lamb and glue on some googly eyes. The straw prints look just like the curly wool of a lamb!

This is a great technique that can also be used for printing fish scales!

Pets and Garden Animals

Fork Print Hedgehog

Materials:

- Brown paper or card
- Brown and black marker pen
- Brown paint
- Fork

On the brown paper draw an outline of a hedgehog. You might want to draw it in pencil first then go over it with pen!

Provide your child with the brown pen (a paper plate is a useful palette for this activity) and show them how to make the spikes of the hedgehog with the back of the fork dipped in paint.

Cover the whole body of the hedgehog with the fork prints!

Experiment with making hedgehogs of different sizes - you could create a whole family!

This technique could be used to recreate other animals too – perhaps the mane of a lion or the fur of a rabbit?

Mouse Finger Puppets

Materials:

- Paper
- Circle template
- Scissors
- Small pom poms
- Googly eyes
- Glue and tape
- Pipe cleaners
- Wire cutters

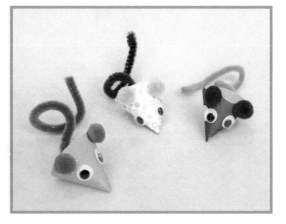

Use the circle template to cut out circles on the paper approximately 3" diameter. Cups or lids work well as templates. Cut the circles in half, then glue the two ends to make a cone. This stage can be a little fiddly so may be best if completed by an adult.

Invite your child to glue on the googly eyes and pom poms for ears.

Cut the pipe cleaners in half using the wire cutters, then tape one half to the inside of the paper cone. Curl it around to form a tail - this will then wrap around your child's finger! These puppets are so fun for pretend play!

Dog Paw Prints

Materials:

- Super thick craft foam or several layers of thin craft foam

- Scissors

- Hot glue gun and glue

- Large bottle cap

- Paper

- Paint or ink

To make the paw print stamper, cut out shapes from a thick piece of craft foam. If using several layers, glue them together first. You will need one larger piece and four smaller pieces. Use a hot glue gun to adhere the craft foam to the top of a bottle cap (a laundry detergent bottle cap was used in the picture below). These stages are jobs for an adult.

Once the glue has set, your child is ready to get stamping! Dip the bottle cap into paint or ink, then press it onto the paper. To clean between colors, simply wipe with a wet cloth or wet paper towel.

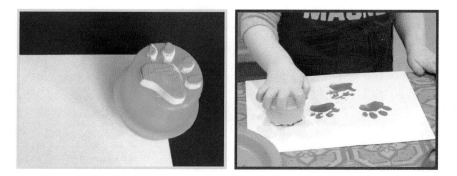

Cardboard Tube Rabbit

Materials:

- Colored card or paper

- Cardboard tube

- White paint

- Glue

- Googly eyes

- White pom pom

Show your child how to dip the end of the cardboard tube into the white paint then stamp it onto the colored card to make two circles.

Then push the sides of the tube together so that a long thin oval shape is formed. Use this to stamp the ears. You may find it useful to tape the top of the tube together to keep the shape.

After the paint has dried, use the glue to add the googly eyes and pom pom tail. You could also draw on extra features like nose, mouth, whiskers and paws.

Fishbowl Craft

Materials:

- White card
- Green and blue tissue paper
- Water and paintbrush
- Scissors
- Grains or sand
- Glue
- Metallic paper

The first stage of this craft is to make the background for the fishbowl. This involves "gluing" pieces of tissue paper to card with water. Fill the card with the tissue paper, brushing water all over, and leave to dry.

When the tissue paper is dry, it will flake off, staining the card with the dye. Cut the card into a fishbowl shape.

Spread glue onto the base of the fishbowl and sprinkle grains or sand all over the glue (cous cous was used in the above picture) *Note: you may need to brush a layer of glue over the top of the grains to fully secure them.*

Cut strips of green tissue paper and glue them on, and add fish cut from the metallic paper.

Handprint Frog

Materials:

- Green card
- Pencil
- Scissors
- Red card
- White card
- Black marker
- Glue

On the green card, trace around your child's hand with the pencil. Cut it out and use it as a template to make a second hand outline in green card.

Cut out a green circle for the frog's body and a long strip of red card for the tongue. Wrap it around the pencil to make it curl up! Make some eyes with the white card and black marker.

Invite your child to glue all the components together. They will especially love playing with the frog's tongue!

This would be a great family or class activity with everyone making their own frog!

Dog Ears Headband

Materials:

- Large white paper
- Brown paint
- Sponge
- Scissors
- Glue
- Tape

Invite your child to paint the paper with the brown paint, using only a sponge. Fingerpaint paper is good for this as its glossy surface causes the sponge to leave lines like fur.

Once the paint has dried, cut out two dog ear shapes and a long band. Wrap the band around your child's head to check it is long enough: you may need to add on extra pieces.

Glue the ears to the band. Roll some tape into a circle (sticky side out) to use as an easy-on-easy-off fastening for the headband.

This headband a lot of fun for some doggy pretend play. Woof!

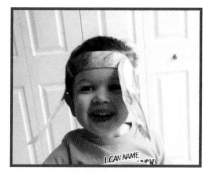

Fluffy Cat Art

Materials:

- White card

- Pencil or printed cat outline

- Yarn (preferably a fluffy kind)

- Scissors

- Glue

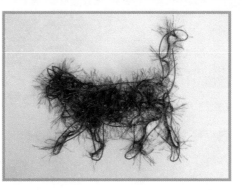

Print out a cat outline onto the white card or draw one freehand. You can easily find animal outlines on the internet.

Cut the yarn into small pieces. This is great fine motor practice if your children are able to use scissors.

Spread glue all over the cat outline and place the yarn onto the glue.

This artwork isn't really about creating the most beautiful picture of a cat - it's about letting your child play with the yarn and encouraging them to fill in the outline just using the yarn.

Depending on the kind of yarn you have you could use this technique to make all kinds of animals!

Birds

Peacock Craft

Materials:

- Colored card
- Blue/green craft sticks
- Glue
- Blue and green feathers
- Blue and yellow craft foam or card
- Scissors
- Googly eye

Glue the craft sticks to the colored card in a fan shape. Depending on the age and ability of the child this may be a job for an adult.

Invite your child to glue the feathers all over the craft sticks.

Cut out a body/head shape from the blue craft foam and a yellow beak. Glue these over the feathers.

Add a googly eye to finish.

Footprint Penguin

Materials:

- Colored card
- Black washable paint
- Paintbrush
- White felt
- Scissors
- Googly eyes
- Glue
- QTips and white paint

Paint your child's foot with the black paint then press it firmly onto the colored card. Paint on some wings.

When the paint has dried, invite your child to glue on the googly eyes, a yellow card triangle for a beak, and a belly cut from the white felt.

To finish the picture, add snow by dipping a QTip into white paint and making dot prints.

Have baby wipes or a damp cloth handy for quick clean up after getting the footprint!

Paper Plate Swan

Materials:

- White paper plate

- Pencil

- Scissors

- Glue

- White feathers

- Googly eye

- Orange marker pen

Use the pencil to draw cutting lines as shown in the above photo. Invite your child to cut out the center section of the plate as marked.

Glue on white feathers to the body and a googly eye to the head.

To finish, color in the beak with an orange pen.

This craft would also work as a goose or duck for a farm theme!

Bottle Cap Birds

Materials:

- Colored card
- Bottle caps
- Glue
- Feathers
- Yellow craft foam or card
- Googly eyes
- Marker pen

Glue the bottle caps to the card in sets of two - preferably a large cap for the body and a smaller cap for the head.

Invite your child to add glue to the caps so that they can glue on feathers to the body, and googly eyes and yellow triangle beaks to the head.

To finish, draw on legs and feet with a marker pen.

Try making other animals or bugs using this technique!

Feathered Bird

Materials:

- Red craft foam
- Scissors
- Background paper
- Glue
- Yellow card or craft foam
- Feathers
- Googly eye

Cut out a basic bird shape from the red craft foam and glue it onto the background paper.

Provide your child with the remaining materials. Depending on their age you can spread glue onto the body of the bird for them or let them do it.

Encourage them to glue the feathers to the bird, and then add the beak (cut from the yellow card) and the eye. Draw on some legs with a marker pen.

Why not try using a range of colored feathers to create new and wonderful birds?!

Swimming Duck

Materials:

- White card

- Pen

- Scissors

- White paper plate

- Blue and yellow paint

- Craft knife and cutting surface

- Craft stick

- Glue

Invite your child to color the paper plate with blue paint. Freehand draw (or print out a template) two ducks onto the white card, one facing left and one facing right. Invite your child to color them with yellow paint.

After the paint has dried, use a craft knife to cut a slit in the paper plate - this is a job for an adult.

Cut out the ducks, and glue them back to back on top of a craft stick. When the glue has dried, insert the craft stick through the slit in the paper plate and let the duck "swim"!

Cardboard Tube Owl

Materials:

- Empty toilet paper tube

- Colored paper

- Glue

- Small feathers

- Googly eyes

Cut out a piece of colored paper to cover the cardboard tube - about 6x4.25" is the right size. Wrap it around the tube and glue it into place.

Push down the top of the tube on one side, then repeat on the opposite side, forming ears. Glue into place.

Provide colored paper cut into wing shapes and beak, plus feathers and googly eyes. Invite your child to glue the parts of the bird onto the tube.

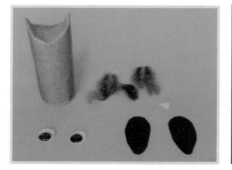

This is a super frugal activity that can be made with leftover scraps of craft materials!

Tissue Paper Duck

Materials:

- Yellow card

- White card

- Scissors

- Tissue paper

- Glue

- Googly eye

Draw an outline of a duck onto the yellow card, either by drawing freehand or by using a template found online. Cut it out and glue it onto the white card.

If your child is old enough to use scissors, invite them to cut the tissue paper up into small pieces. Otherwise you can do this for them.

Use the glue to adhere the tissue paper pieces to the duck. This is really easy for even young children to do! A glue stick could be used instead of white glue to minimize mess. Finish by adding a googly eye.

This technique can be used to make pictures of any kind of animal, bird or insect!

Play Dough Birds

Materials:

- Play dough (see page 34)

- Feathers

- Googly eyes

- Drinking straws

- Scissors

- Yellow craft foam

Cut the straws into small lengths and the craft foam into triangles. Older children can help with this - cutting straws can be a lot of fun!

Mold the play dough into balls and encourage your child to push the feathers into the ball.

Then push in the eyes, the yellow craft foam beak and the straws (to form legs).

One of the great things about this craft is that children can make new birds by just removing all the items and starting again on a new creation.

Why not try making play dough turkeys for a fun Thanksgiving themed activity?!

Bugs and Insects

Foam Ball Spider

Materials:

- 3" Styrofoam balls*
- Black paint
- Paint brush
- Pipe cleaners
- Wire cutters
- Googly eyes
- Glue

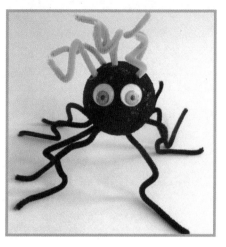

You can use either the hard smooth type or the softer rough type of ball for this craft. The hard type is easier to paint, but the soft type is easier to push pipe cleaners into!

Invite your child to paint the Styrofoam ball with black paint. Washable paint is a good idea here as this can get rather messy!

When the paint has dried, show your child how to push the pipe cleaners into the ball. Pipe cleaners have sharp ends so supervise your child at all times. If you need to cut the pipe cleaners, use wire cutters (NOT scissors!) Bend the pipe cleaners to form legs. Glue on some googly eyes to finish.

These spiders are really fun to make for Halloween!

Coffee Filter Paper Butterflies

Materials:

- Coffee filter papers

- Marker pens

- Eye dropper and water

- Scissors

Open out the filter papers and encourage your child to scribble on them with marker pens. It may be useful to tape the filters to the table.

Once they have finished coloring, give them the eye dropper with some water so that they can sprinkle it onto the filter paper. You don't need much water for the colors to run into each other and create pretty patterns.

When they have dried, cut out butterfly shapes and add in extra details with the pens. A whole group of them looks very pretty!

This technique is a pretty way to make flowers, too!

Craft Stick Caterpillar

Materials:

- Craft sticks

- Glue

- Pom poms in two sizes

- Googly eyes

Show your child how to spread glue onto a craft stick. Encourage them to place pom poms onto the glue, with a larger pom pom at one end to form the head. Make sure they push the pom poms right down onto the craft stick to help them adhere.

Glue on the googly eyes.

Extend this craft to a pattern-matching activity by preparing one in advance and asking your child to copy the same color pom poms as you have chosen.

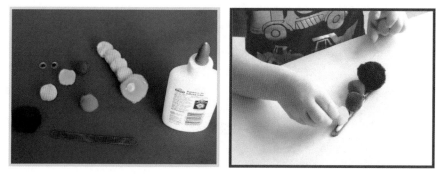

Snail Suncatcher

Materials:

- Tissue paper
- Scissors
- Contact paper
- Tape
- Marker pens
- Colored card
- Pipe cleaner

Cut the tissue paper into small pieces. If your child can use scissors then they can help with this!

Peel the backing off the Contact paper and tape it to the table, sticky side up. Provide your child with the tissue paper and show them how it attaches without any glue!

Cover the tissue paper with another layer of Contact paper, sticky sides together. Cut out a snail shell shape. Cut out a snail body shape from the colored card. Glue the shell to the body and add details with marker pen.

Bend a pipe cleaner in half and tape it to the back to form the tentacles.

> **Even the youngest of toddlers can put tissue paper onto Contact paper!**

Paper Plate Bumblebee

Materials:

- Yellow paper plate

- Painters' tape

- Black paint

- Googly eye

- Black tulle or tissue paper

- Glue

Prepare the plate by using the tape to mark stripes across it.

Leaving the tape in place, invite your child to paint the whole of the plate with black paint. Paintbrushes are optional!

When the paint has dried, carefully remove the tape to reveal the striped body of the bee.

Cut out some wings from the black tulle (or tissue paper) and glue them onto the back of the plate, then add a googly eye.

This style of painting is called "tape resist" and is perfect for toddlers!

Cupcake Liner Butterflies

Materials:

- Clothespins

- Paint

- Standard cupcake liners

- Mini cupcake liners

- Scissors

- Glue

- Glitter glue (optional)

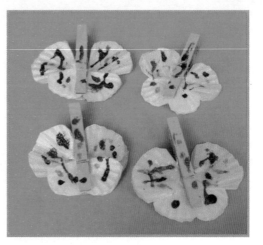

Paint the clothespins and leave to dry. For each butterfly you'll need two standard size and two mini cupcake liners. Fold each one into quarters. Glue them into pairs that include one of each size.

Trim the corners off each folded cupcake liner to look more like the shape of a butterfly wing.

Clip the two sets of wings together with the clothespin.

Older children may be able to get involved with the stages above, younger children may just like to help color the butterflies. Glitter glue works well or paint dabbed on with QTips.

The craft featured in the photos uses white cupcake liners - but you could use printed ones instead!

Watercolor and Glue Ladybugs

Materials:

- Hot glue gun and glue

- White card

- Watercolor paints

- Water

- Paintbrushes

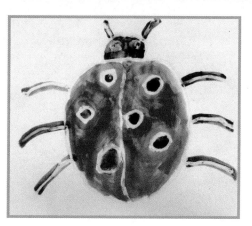

This craft needs some adult preparation in advance. Use a hot glue gun to draw the outline and basic details of the ladybug onto the white card.

Invite your child to paint the ladybug with the watercolor paints. They will discover that they cannot paint on the glue! An interesting effect is then created as they try and paint around the glue.

You could also try this craft using some light colored card instead of white to produce a different effect.

This technique works well for other bugs too: try butterflies, snails or caterpillars!

Inchworm Craft

Materials:

- Pipe cleaners

- Wire cutters

- Pony beads

- Googly eyes

- Glue

Cut each pipe cleaner in half using the wire cutters. To start the activity, thread one pony bead onto the pipe cleaner and twist over the end to hold it in place. Then hand it over to your child and invite them to thread on more beads.

They could make patterns by alternating bead colors, use one just color, or completely random!

Leave a little space at the end and curl it round to form a head shape - this will also hold all the beads in place. Glue some tiny googly eyes to each side of the head, then bend the pipe cleaner into the classic inchworm shape!

This craft is also great fine motor practice for little hands!

INDEX

About the Author

Georgina is originally from the UK but is now living in the US with her husband and son. She starting crafting with her son when he was just one year old, and created the blog *Craftulate* so that she could share their art, crafts and activities with others. She is also the author of the book *Art, Craft and Cooking with Toddlers* and co-author of the book *99 Fine Motor Ideas*.

Made in the USA
Lexington, KY
18 March 2016